On A Clear Night,
A Star Shines.

It Beckons.

Come Listen,
Come Journey.

To Susl
   with much affection
      from celia
          9/06

Printed in USA by
Signature Book Printing, Inc.
Gaithersburg, MD 20879
www.sbpbooks.com

ISBN 0-9663311-0-9

First Printing   August 2002

Dedicated to

My Beloved

and

to all

whose paths

have mingled with mine

along The Way.

Table of Contents

Illustrations

Glossary

Shechina: Transliteration of the Hebrew for God's indwelling presence, conceived as feminine.

Miriam: Sister of Moses who played her tamborine after crossing the Red Sea.

Elijah: He who will usher in the Messiah

D'Varim: Deuteronomy, the fifth book of the Hebrew Bible

Shema, Yisrael: "Listen, O Israel" - from Deuteronomy 6:4

Shabbos: The commanded day of rest - Shabbat, Sabbath

HaShem: the word to replace the unknowable, unsayable name of the One.

Mezuzah: Hebrew for door posts. Also the small container placed on the doorposts of Jewish homes which holds a copy of the Shema.

Traveler

I am
a dusty traveler,
an explorer, I would say,
on a long,
evolving journey.

This is a special place,
this stop
along the way.
How long I will be here
I cannot say.
I bring to you
the best
of who I have become.
You give to me
the best
of who you are.

When I move along,
I shall not leave you,
for you will be
a part
of who I am
along
the way.

Inner Peace

Travel lightly
and you will journey endlessly
yet never tire.

Sleep with compassion
and you will never sleep alone
or wake in pain.

Ride the storm with faith
and it will bring you
to the quiet side.

Cast your soul to the wind
to find its true way
and it will come back to you
blessed by all the elements of life.

Psalm

Life of all life,
the Creator of all creation,
guides me, provides for me.
I shall not want.

I am led to the depths
of my inner darkness,
to where the knowing
that I have forgotten lies.
I am led to rest, to meditate,
to receive guidance
by reconnecting with my Soul.

Yea, though I walk through the valley
of the shadow of Death,
through my own darkness,
seeing my own imperfections,
Thy teachings and protection comfort me.
I shall fear no evil.
I have what I need
in spite of the doubts that plague me.
I have what I want; I lack nothing.-
all the days of my life,
and I shall be alive with Life of all life,
and with Death of all death,
Creator creating,
One Being,
One and All always.

<u>Journey</u>

Together we have forged many an uncharted territory
and survived the perils of their wilderness. I realize I
am tired from the struggles, and an overwhelming
weariness slips about me as we come to the edge of a
rocky, precipitous cliff.

"I would like so to stop here and rest," I say. "You
may rest a moment so long as the whole while you are
thinking of Me," is whispered in the wind. My very
being is penetrated and I shiver as I stare into the thick
clouds covering the cavern below. I try to warm myself
with memories of awe and my deep thanks for the
bounty which has been bestowed upon me as I have
seen my cup repeatedly filled. With each peak we have
climbed, I have been transformed by the view.

Yet as I look down into the valley below, I feel fearfully
inadequate to descend again. Silently, my gaze is led
ahead to still another brilliant peak, and I know we must
go down in order further to climb. This descent into the
murkiness below will be the more frightening, for once
begun I shall see neither what is below nor above. So,
too, the direction of the climb more unsure, yet, in the
end, exhilarating, for I have seen glimpses of Your
rewards. But, now, in my tiredness and weariness, I fear
I will lose my way and not have the strength to find the
path. I feel I will be besieged by inner armies that can
destroy me.

"Yes, you could indeed, that is why I Am with you. Put your faith truly in Me, and I will guide the way and allow none to defeat you. Until you can make the journey as one with Me, I will lead you. But as long as you follow Me, we will climb ever higher and struggle ever more until we move as One. Rest now. Rest, for in the dawn we begin again.

As I close my eyes and breath deeply of the air graced by the All Being, I feel the strength within me begin gently to rekindle; and the small flame begins to soften the shadows of fear.

Praying

To whom do I pray
now that I know
All is not only there
but also here?

How do I pray
now that I see
All is not only what Is,
but also what I Am?

Why would I pray
when I feel
the Dark and the Light
are One
and The One
is with me always?

I know not.
But marveling at
the voices of angels
singing softly within,
I pray,
giving thanks.

Winter Solstice

Day of longest night,
from hence the sun's light
again increases.
Yet the darkness deepens.

The candle flickers.
The shadows dance.
Breath deeply the sweet smell of incense.
The music of singing flute
and wind blown chimes fill the air.
The crystal reflects the flickering light.

Walk with me to the depths of my soul,
to the darkest corner.
Bring it to the light that I may see.
Let me not be blinded by fear
or arrogance;
but with humility and the light of love,
bring forth my Self to the light.

There, I will be reborn, changed again,
ready for a new season
after the long dark night.

An Icy Day

Though white cold still pierces this earth,
and my feet are tossed mercilessly aside
for the hard, unyielding ground
to shock my Raggedy-Anne body,
I know there is a season yet to come.
The buds are swelling with their faith in it.
Then there will be a new softness in the earth.
Thawed by the warmth of the increasing sun,
fresh footprints
will mark the passage
of steps
more steadily taken.

Faith

I shall listen to the trees.
Their tips are pregnant with faith
in a season yet to come.
Though the earth is pierced with cold,
they trust in re-birth.
So shall I.

8

Heart Song

There is a song in my heart that longs to be sung.
I hear a few notes in the colors of the clouds.
I hear a melody with the passing of the wind.
It bursts forth in full symphony
when you are embracing me.

My Spirit

My spirit is always dancing.
It twirls within me.
Colors swirling,
it cares not that it is not seen.
Yet longing to be part
of everyone and everything,
faster, faster,
the colors swirl,
blending, blurring,
yet ever more brilliant.

I have found my Beloved!

My Drum

The drum in my soul is pounding loudly.
It calls me.
It calls me.
Too long have I not heard it's song.

Beating, beating, beating.
It was drowned by sounds
now dead, dead, dead.

I can hear it's rhythmic call.
Pounding softly.
Pounding loudly.

It drums into my head.
It drums into my feet.
It drums into my hands.
It drums into my heart.
It drums into my life.

A beating, beating, beating sound
waiting for me to move.

It beats all seasons.
It beats all cycles.
I hear it now
I join it now.

Play it.
Dance it.
Sing it.
Drum it.

All along the rest of my path
from night to day,
from hill to hill,
from star to star,
from heart to soul and back again.

Beat, beat, beat my drum!
I Am Alive!

Dancing

I am dancing.
I am dancing.
I am dancing, dancing, dancing.

Drums are pounding.
Drums are pounding.
Voices chanting,
I am dancing.

Arms fling high.
Arms swing low.
Colors swirling,
round they go.
I am dancing.
I am dancing, dancing, dancing.

Head tossed back.
Foot kicked high.
Skirt twirling,
round I go.

Tambourine jangling.
Tapping head,
Tapping hand,
Tapping hip,
jangling, jangling, jangling.

I am dancing.
I am dancing.
I am leaping.
I am flying.

It may seem
that I am driving.
It may seem
that I am cleaning.
It may seem
that I hold a child.

But, I am dancing.
I am dancing.
I am dancing, dancing, dancing.

Longing

Deep in my soul
there is a song to be sung,
a prayer to be said,
a tear to be wiped,
a love to be shared.

A longing more vast than all
that I know and don't know is there.
I can only begin to fill it
with the trusting smile of a child,
with the gaze of my love's eyes,
and with the opening of my heart
to you.

On A Hill

I came here to rest
gentle breeze.
My strings are taut.
Play, gentle breeze,
play carefully.

On The Mountain

I came here to sit a while,
alone at the top of a mountain.
For it is here that I find You,
where we have met before.

In the heat of the sun
reflected from the bare rock,
in the strength of the wind
suddenly whistling
across the open cliff face,
in the expanse of the view
carrying colors into infinity.
You once again fill me.

Brimming forth,
knowing is renewed.
There is no "alone."
There is instead
tremendous "Oneness"
with the vastness of life,
and I drink deeply
from Your cup once again.

Despair

Despair
cannot ride for long
the moving crest of the wave
in the moonlight,
but is crashed below
and churned about
until it rises again
as Courage,
glistening in the sunlight.

As the sun and moon
dance together in the sky,
as the sea and sand
sing boisterously,
as the mind and heart
struggle for unity,
so does Courage
journey with Despair,
pulling and pushing
to define its strength,
to know its
power,
then to yield all
willingly
in order to be
reborn as Faith.

Wholeness

Quiet pool,
though gently lands the swan,
the reflection is broken.
Yet you comfort me,
for not only do you mend,
but add the image of the swan as well.

Rebirth

What beach
will I next be cast upon?

Will I glide forth
as a polished shell,
having given up life,
to be a smooth bit of color
in someone's hand?

Will I then be dropped,
to roll silently out again
to the churning depths?

Will I be tossed to the shore,
spit forth by the storm
battered and broken?

Will I be a gnarled and twisted piece,
unrecognizable,
yet firmly stuck in the sand,
blanketed
by the fury of the wind?

As I am
will I be found
and unknown beauty
and new purpose
recognized?

Will I be a reminder then
that, in truth,
death is nonexistent?

Seeking God

I do not know when I began looking for
God. I remember feeling very close to the All
Knowing One as a child, praying fervently to
be able to do His bidding. Yet somewhere,
sometime, we parted ways. It seems a very
long time now that I have been seeking to find
The Source of All Life again. I have caught
glimpses from time to time and felt a tremendous
joy of reunion, only to have It go again, or so it
seemed. I have wanted so to know The One,
to understand All, to be at one with One, to return
to Transcendence as I was in my childhood. I have
been seeking far and wide and seen many
representations of Her face and yet could not find
myself closer.

Now, I am coming to the awareness that
to want to know and understand All That Is comes
from a desire of the mind which serves the Ego.
When God is seen through the eyes of Faith, which
is of the heart and spirit, then I see that The One is
everywhere and always has been. It is the clouds
of doubt, which are also of the mind, which darken
the lens of Faith.

I pray for the strength to let go of the need
to control;
I pray for the courage to let go of fear.
For these block the flow of compassion
that springs from the well of Faith.
I pray for this healing
for myself as well as all others.
In drinking from the cup filled with
Compassion, my Faith is renewed.
In renewing my Faith, once again I see God,
and I am filled with joy!

Clouds

When I was young, the clouds beckoned
with illusive shapes.
There were towering castles and hidden lands
of giants with capes.
There were sweeping ships to ride and friendly beasts
to chase.

Great, billowing pillows offered places in which to hide.
My innocent child's mind, created inner chambers,
softly filled with color
of a most opalescent kind,
where no-one's eyes ever cried.

As young dreams dissolved in the rain showers of time,
the colors muted and faded.
The clouds drifted from view,
carried by the storms to the mountain's far side.
Tears filled my inner child's eye.

But the mountain called and the upward journey began,
driven by dreams, challenged by reality,
I traversed many a steep trail, rounded many a bend.

24

The wind at the peak bid me to look up again.
High, high, where there was no-one else to hail,
clouds billowed brilliantly in a deep blue sky,
not one too pale!

But now, there was no need to dream
of castles or kings,
or to ride imaginary ships,
or horses with wings.
I felt the breeze that moved the clouds
caress my face.
Dazzled, I watched the towering puffs
gently cross this space
into a new mind in this expansive sky,
where mountains and clouds heralded a new
view of life.

Moon Pearl

The moon is full.
My soul is full.
My spirit floats in a sea of joy and wonder.
Patience my heart.
I must stop and listen a while.
To play.
To delight in being.
To hear the music of the spheres.
To stare into the waters lit by this soft light.
To touch the beams below and above.
To rest in the cool glow. Then up I go!
To ride the night in the round chariot,
carried gently across the sky, through the deep waters
where earth and spirit are one.
Patience my heart.
I will return.

Here, where I stand, the grass is heavy with dew,
soaking my sneakers, feet and trousers through.
The wet droplets sparkle in the cool light.
A milky mist drifts across the road,
hangs low upon the field and hovers, hugging the trees.
A few dark silhouettes can be seen here and there.
A shrub, the top of the old oak and pine.
The grasses along the edge of the fence.
The shroud softly, silently drifts.

Above is a deep indigo crystal clarity.
A sea of dark silk showing off its luminous pearl
and a single diamond.
As the oyster's pearl covers pain, the moon,
shining with cool bright beauty,
hides the dark side of ours.

Walking with the moon, alone, I see the light,
but know in my depths the dark is there.
Come again, luminous chariot, take me for a ride
when the dark is full,
and the light but a sliver.
I know that I will I shiver,
for the drifting clouds and the dew drops
will not be seen,
only the wetness, the dampness felt.
Then if the rides repeat,
through the cycles of her times,
I again will see the fullness of the bright side.
Having spent time with her darkness,
the luminous will be more complete and whole.

Metamorphosis

I died.
The pain was deep
as I was dashed against the rocks
by the pounding surf.
I slid to the bottom of the sea.
There, resting on the sand,
I rocked in the darkness
with the gentle rhythms
of the sea,
seeing nothing,

yet knowing,
Life was everywhere.

Surrounded by Life,
slowly I was lifted up again
towards the building waves.
I surged forth in the bubbles
singing on the sand,
shimmering in the sunlight.
I died,
and was reborn.

Meetings

I love the way you come,
and I love the way you go.
In your face I see the light
of The One who makes us whole.

I love the way you welcome me,
and the way you bid me leave.
Through the openness of your heart,
flows Shechina's love.

The space and time in which we meet
is boundless yet containing.
Whether we arrive or whether we leave,
our journey is blessed within its mystery.

I love the way you come,
and I love the way you go.
May the song in our hearts
and the tune from our lips
mingle with the Breath of Life
passing in, through, and amongst us.

I love the way you welcome me,
and the way you bid me leave.
As our paths cross and cross again,
may the enlarging space within us
embrace where we were, are,
and have yet to be.

I love the way you come,
and I love the way you go.

Only Your Self

Is there no one who can know
the depth of your sorrow?
No one who can see
the breadth of your despair?
Is there no one who feels
the sharpness of your pain?
No one with whom to cross
the chasm of your fears?

Do you feel that no one is with you
as in the darkness you crumble,
no one?

Ah, but I believe
that there is.....
Deep in the shadows, buried
deep in the hole of loneliness, waiting,
is a small voice, a flickering flame.

The Source of your Life,
the spark which is made
in the image of God,
waits for the blackness to be defied
by your stare,
to shatter it into fragments
that reflect new brilliance and color.

Then you will be free
to soar with Love and Compassion.

No one else can touch.
No one else can reach.
No one else can bring it forth.
No one.

But, having traveled the depth
of your darkness,
you can dare
to be your Self.

You can walk with your Light
by the Sea of Life
where it matters not
if footprints remain in the sand.

Time

Time brings an increased awareness,
a growing understanding,
a softening of pain,
a gentling of moments gone awry,
an increased balance
of hope and cynicism.

Time is
life ever living,
love ever giving,
souls ever moving
on the continuum of changes
and circles of lives intertwined.

Time is
a mirror and yet a blank page.
Where we have come from
can be on the other side of where we are going.

In this time,
we are at a crossing of roads,
a turning towards new paths.
As we look towards evolving decisions,
may the roads chosen pass through
times of joy and sharing,
reflecting a love both given and received,
to transcend these times
for times as yet undefined.

36

Pondering

If I ponder
what "might have been,"
tears
of self-centeredness
drown my spirit.

If I ponder
what "will be,"
apprehension immobilizes
me.

Pondering
what "is"
in the darkness of fears
and seeming imperfections
dulls my senses.

Living
what "is"
by the clear, bubbling waters
of Grace and Gratitude,
I am enriched,
and
what "will be"
"is,"
and "might have been"
matters not.

Winter Walk

The path through the woods
is strewn with icy puddles and slippery rocks
that threaten to throw my feet skyward
and my derriere down.
The limbs of the birch trees drip cold wetness
against my neck.
Bits of snow drop, splattering my coat.

Picking my way through the thick fog,
I exhilarate in the adventure of quietly slipping
into a seemingly magical land
of moist, sweet-smelling coldness.
Blurred images suddenly crisp, then gone again,
blend with my imagination.

My spirit feels its burden of pain and sorrow
dissolving
as my body, willingly and laughingly,
accepts the challenge
of ice, snow, and softly clouded view.
Cautiously my footprints crunch the crystalline snow
and my breath hangs in the air before me.

The narrow path turns into an open meadow.
At the hilltop the snow glistens blindingly
in the sun, brightly reflecting
blue shadows of delicately slumbering trees.

Breathing deeply the cool moist air,
I feel myself moving
to a different place within,
and I am relieved.

Seagull and I

Ah, to be the
spot of sunlight
flashing upon your breast,
to feel the wind pushing
past my sensibilities!

Is it your apparent
inaccessibility
which stirs the poem
in my heart?
Is it the ascending flight
of your winged beauty
which uplifts
my Soul?

Deeply
I feel the brilliant soaring
of the gull wheeling
joyfully in the warm sun.
My spirit clings
to the flashing feathers,
the more dazzling
because of the depth
of the blue
into which they fly.

Suddenly,
my body feels not the earth
beneath its feet,
but the rushing air
and sun's heat
and a surging
toward a height
incomprehensible!

The Beach

Shhh!
The song of my drummer is soft.
The sound of the waves is soothing,
reflecting the gentle rhythm.
The dawn is joyful.
The clear beach invites my feet
to wander freely,
unfettered.
Footprints run in and out of the
simmering water's edge.
Whose are they?
The sun of the new day
warms me.
The sand oozes between my toes,
inviting them to dig in
and add mine
to the design!

The Rock and The Wave.

My own laughter
explodes from within me
as I stand in the high wet splashes
of the happy wave
that hugged the rocks too hard!

The water breaks
into a thousand glittering bits
pelting hard and cold
upon my skin.

Falling away
it bubbles and sings,
blending and rebuilding,
to crescendo forth playfully again.

It leaves me breathlessly exuberant.
For a timeless moment,
I have been a partner
in the dance
of the rock and the wave.

Birthdays

1.

It's your birthday.
I'm glad you came my way.
You have traveled roads I shall never see,
and you walk on paths down which
I can only glance.
I treasure, then, those places where
we sit for a while,
passing time together.
It's your birthday,
and I am pleased
and enriched
to know some of you.

2.

As days and nights
and sorrows and joys
weave the tapestry of your life,
may the tensions be balanced
to form a strong fabric
with bright colors.
Blessed and bound
with a fringe firmly tied
by the Holy Weaver,
may the wearing of it
warm your Soul.

3.

As the wheel within spins 'round
auguring another year
of hopes, dreams and challenges,
and conquering of fears,
my gift to you,
from deep within my sensibilities,
is a place of comfort
with the door left ajar.

4.

The passage of time
Brings unpredictable changes,
Some brought by our own means,
some by forces unseen.
The body fails us more and more;
the mind ponders things
unknowable before.
The cycles of our lives
continually spiral round
until within ourselves
new dimensions are found.
In the passage of time,
in the seasons lived,
we learn about Love
and the blessings it gives.
In celebrating your birth,
celebrate your life,
and all that has passed before
that manifests now in who you are
and the life you live.

In Your Absence

I miss you gently.
For that I am glad.
To feel any less
would leave me empty;
to feel any more,
would leave me sad.

You and *I*

You were the rock
midstream
greeting my bubbling
waters.
Though I could not
stay with you,
with you I sang
as I went by.

Letting Go

The wind blew your name to me,
a soft memory
causing only the curtains to flutter.
It brushed gently from one window,
through another,
and then flew free.

In Passing

We passed,
you and I,
as brown and crimson leaves
floating on the breeze,
skipping o'er the ground.
Perhaps,
in another season,
we could have lingered longer.
Perhaps.

The Bridge

The bridge beckons you;
But slowly cross.
Let yourself feel the gentle curve
of time through space.

Pause for awhile
mid-span,
letting past and future
softly blend.

In that moment of now,
take in also the beauty
of above and below.

Feel yourself in a place
where earth, air, and water
meet the fire of life
and become one with you.

Being yourself whole,
freely you go on.

Spring Day

It's a spring day!
My spirit flies to a tree top
there to nestle in a blossom
tickled by the warm sun.

A Wish

When I gaze up at the clear night sky,
I long to be there amongst the stars.
I cannot fathom the distance that they really are.
I want to step from one to the other,
gathering sparkling light
and sprinkling it on the earth below,
increasing the brightness
of every earthbound soul.

Old Friend

Old friend, I wonder where you are.
Images of you drift into my mind from time to time.
They are out of date now, I am certain.
For I have changed and surely so have you.
Our paths are different, yours and mine,
yet we each know something
of the other's way.
Our destinies have parted our footprints,
sending them on opposite beams,
yet in some unknown time and place,
as they circle round,
they will come again to you and me.
Do my thoughts of you
find their way into your dreams
so that an image of me
might be seen?
Your face is young still,
for memories know nothing
of time or age.
I pray that the earth you touch,
and the fruit and flower you bring forth,
may nurture your soul.

Paths

The crossing of our paths
has been a joy to me,
and I shall remember you.
The mingling of the colors of our lives
has woven luminous threads,
soft and warm,
to wrap 'round my soul

My Young Friend

Your beautiful gifts and talents
are given and blessed by Grace.
You shall travel roads rich
with meaning in Life.
I am deeply honored
that you have invited me
to walk with you a while.
I shall go with you as far as I can.
Then I shall watch you spread your wings
and soar;
and when you call to me,
I shall hear your voice on the wind.

The Tree And I

How tall this tree
and so strong.
What wisdom flows within?
How willingly it shelters
and supports me.
What message do I hear
softly whispering?

Quietly I listen,
eyes closed,
back pressed against
this gnarled but solid form.
Breathing easily
with the flow of the wind
across my face,
I feel my soul pulled deeply below
and then stretched infinitely above.

Suddenly I am one with this tree,
pushing firmly along the roots,
into the earth,
yet soaring high
with the branches in the breeze.
Strength fills my body.
Yet I am floating.

When it is time to leave,
to allow the separation,
there is a sense of physical loss,
but only momentarily.
The senses have been permanently
changed.

Within,
I have only to close my eyes
in the dancing wind,
or climb to the top of the hill,
to touch its source again.

A Complete Day

Contains
some work well done,
a task completed,
a project begun.

Preserves
a moment of rest,
of thoughts turned inward,
deepening, expanding,
as the soul reflects.

Presents
something new
or differently viewed,
something learned
or more clearly understood.

Finds
a special beauty touched,
a love once again expressed,
a precious moment
of thankfulness.

Yields
a chance to give,
to make someone smile,
or to create
a moment
of peaceful joy.

May expose
a tear,
or momentary confusion,
or an expression
of painful sorrow.

Rebounds
with a faithful perception
of the sweet evening
containing hope
for another day
and another conversation
with G-d.

Life's Fire

The fire has been started
with images
of what might have been.

Let the flames dance higher still
on images
of what has been.

The bright warmth of these last offerings
bathe my Soul
cleansing it
for images that are.

No need to fuel the coals
with images
of what will be.

The beauty of the flickering flames
joins the heat
of the deepening embers.
The fire burns long
and deeply warms me.

Together

Can humility and joy
dance together?
Can bent knee and bowed head
take part in the leaping, twirling
rhythms of Life?

Can the stillness
of standing in one spot,
eyes closed, palms open,
burst forth
into the pirouette and raised arms
that move with the beating drum?

Surely as the silent silver light
of the moon glides along
the surf that crashes on the shore,
the shared dance is all that there is.

Love

To be loved
by my friend
with whom I share
memorable times,
is a great gift
to be treasured.
But to be loved
by one
with whom
I differ and disagree,
is to be blessed
by the Grace of God.

To love my friend
is a personal joy.
To love one
who travails me
is to release
my Soul in song.
For in the end,
it is he
who shows me
the truth
concerning Love.

For You

May the strength and courage of all
great women be with you.
May the compassion
of The All Knowing One
sustain your heart.
May the shoulders
of The Great Beloved
carry you through.

May you have a warm and cozy
winter and a blessed renewal
come spring.

May the warmth of your smile
always brighten
the heart of another.

Blessed be your spirit,
Peaceful be your heart,
Warm be your hearth,
and joyful be your walk.

Have a cheerful and warm spring,
filled with color and song
and renewal of Life.

Contrasts

Here am I in a world of contrasts
and yet it is the contrasts
that exemplify all of Life.
They are a continuum really,
a circular one,
a spiraling one,
moving into and out of one another.
> Where there is light, there is darkness.
> Where there is beauty, there is desolation.
> Where there is understanding, there is ignorance.
> Where there is love, there is rage.
> Where there is peace, there is war.
> Where there is generosity, there is greed.
> Where there is life, there is death.
> Where there is creation, there is destruction.
> Where there is healing, there is pain.

I stand here on these continuums, and more, knowing that I cannot see the one without the other, as all of Life turns and evolves, each one through the other. Let me not deny or refuse the darkness in favor of the light. Rather, let me walk in the shadows bearing a beacon within that lights the way. This is the human path. It is we who see the opposites, the polarities, humans who are of God but cannot know The Mind. God, however, is One and All, and All is God, who is One.

In The Center

In walking the path of Life,
we may discover that there is no light
without darkness;
that in facing fear, courage is found;
that in seeing hatred,
one values the gift of love;
that in accepting death,
one may begin to live.
In walking the path of Life,
when we come to see these
not as pairs of opposites,
but as a continuum upon which we travel,
and even pause,
then we will come to the center,
which is Compassion.

Sage

It takes a great deal of strength
and discipline,
as well as knowledge of one's self,
for Ego to be replaced by Compassion.
Living with Compassion, Tolerance,
and Patience,
gives the Self boundless freedom
and peace.
It can be one's life work to accomplish
and one's mission to pass it on.

Awareness

It is when one is face to face with Death
that one is most aware of Life.
In the moment that one acknowledges
one's mortality,
one may begin to live.

Musings

Fear is what I hear when I listen to the eternal scream.
Life is what I see in the fullness of the I Am that is within.
Walking with God at the edge of the pounding sea,
Faith replaces fear.

When I danced with my shadow, the fire burned brightly.

Desiring perfection one never exists.
Perfection is death itself,
so blank pages stay blank.

As the clouds part, letting the rays behind pour through,
I am reminded that it is behind the darkness
that the light is brightest.

In the Rain

It used to be
that rain
was merely wetness
upon my cheek,
an annoyance to be avoided,
a bumbershoot projected against.
Nowadays,
it is a sweet "hello!",
a luscious nurturing of the earth,
leaving my own senses
refreshed and cleansed!

Dearly Beloved,

Together we fly through the
textures of changing seasons.
Together we discover
new depths of ourselves,
each other, and the world around us.
Together we keep our hearts warm
and our spirits light.
Together we play and laugh;
we look and touch;
we share the tender place of no time,
no space.
With you in my life,
I find the meaning of Love.

When She Said "Good-bye"

She took my hands
ever so gently,
looking deeply
into my eyes.

She said not a word,
but held us there,
in a moment
of pure being.

There in her face,
I saw the light of God,
and was left with longing.

Yet the moment
is captured in my heart,
to return to
when my mind is still

Longing Again

Longing to merge with Perfection,
to be one with the Light,
can mysteriously plunge one
into a dark pit of despair.

In this life, one may be with the Light
but cannot stay there,
for to do so would burn one out.
Time in the cool, dark shadows
allows room for the light
to re-enter
and for Life to be re-born.
During our time in the realm of hours
and opposites,
we must learn to re-kindle the memory
within our heart
of the Light before Time and its Unity.
Then we may walk in shadows
and through pain
knowing that we Are One.

My Beloved

My beloved's eyes are dark, as dark as still pools
in the night.
Within them lies a deep mystery
that draws me in.
It is a place unfathomable to the mind
but known by the heart.
The depths behind the dark luminosity
glow in his gaze,
and I linger there to drink the sweetness.

My beloved's mouth is tender,
murmuring words of affection,
sharing a loving smile.
Honey sweet lips caress,
savoring the wine
of blessed awe.
My beloved's embrace envelopes me,
merges with me.
We flow in a timeless, infinite unity,
rising with the sparks
released by the Great Love.

My beloved's love dances with mine,
and we know each other
from a time before,
from a oneness with the Source of all Love.
He has been given to me, and I to him,
to worship and manifest together
the All Being through our Love.
The angels rejoice in our knowing.
The playing of harps and the singing of songs
surround our bed of lovemaking.
I see in the gaze of my beloved's dark eyes
the light of a great mystery.

<u>Daring</u>

One of the very few childhood memories I
have of my father is accompanying him to the rocky
shores of the northern Atlantic Ocean. There, I
scampered over the boulders, laughing when the
crashing waves splashed over me. I stopped now
and then to listen to the thwock-swish, thwock-swish
of the water tirelessly, endlessly carving caverns into
the granite beneath my feet. I don't remember much
about him. I only know he was there.

I believe that those precious moments are
at the root of my love for adventure and for dancing
with the powerful forces of nature. There is something
about taking a risk, about facing danger and one's
fears, of even challenging death, that is absolutely
life affirming.

I have recollections of many such experiences
throughout my life journey. Such as balancing a pack
on my back while crawling across a log spanning a
rushing river, or clinging to a rocky cliff over an incoming
tide and anxiously holding my breath just before coaxing
my body up over the edge, even of staring down a brown
bear who was staring down me. I remember the strain of
being in the midst of foaming rapids, delicately urging a
fully loaded canoe to slip from its hard-stuck perch on a
rock, and the enthusiasm of standing deliberately on a
deserted beach in a storm, letting the surging waves grab
at my legs, while I yelled with the pounding of the sea.
It's like daring to come face to face with G-d.

My favorite dare happened one evening
while I was standing on the top of a grassy hill,
the kind of high, clear knoll that's perfect for kite
flying. I watched the color of the sky turn,
peacefully, from pale blue to the electric yellow
that portends a thunder storm. The eerie glow
silently advanced, transforming the deep jade of
the earth to an amber hue. Cumulus clouds,
swelling in darkness and height, gathered
ominously on the hill across from me.
Birds suddenly flocked and swirled, piercing the
stillness with their riotous calls. My dogs,
restless, stayed close to my feet. The increasing
wind tugged and pushed at us, whistling in the
trees around the clearing. A few drops of rain
splattered here and there in warning. People
below us scurried to their cars, rolled up their
windows and drove away. Then the birds,
hidden now, were hushed. I became aware of the
great curve of the earth beneath my feet, felt it
stretching far away to its other side below me.
Together we were spinning through the Universe.
Left alone, alone with the curving, turning earth,
as the front formed in the heavens, from within
my depths a defiance was tempted. I waited and
watched. The electricity in the air increased then
burst forth, zigging here and there, followed by
the crashing

crescendo of the cymbals of thunder. How long could I stand there, rooted to that hill top? How close could I let the tumult come? Exhilaration took my breath away and I felt giddy. I felt I was in the company of the All Mighty and the protection of my ancestors. Perhaps they were even speaking to me. For the moment, I was invincible.

The wetness, the wind, the flashing swords of fire encroached, pursued by the rumbling rolling from hill to hill. The air was drenched with an earthy, pungent sweetness. My bodily senses were quickened and engulfed. My Soul, cut loose and freed, soared as captain of the concourse. Time was trampled, destroyed; Infinite Oneness, triumphant.

With a rush, my sensibilities returned as I began to be seriously pelted by down pouring rain. I let it soak my face before yielding. Turning, rather reluctantly, with the dogs pulling ahead, I, too, darted down the hill to our car, laughing and whooping all the way!

Let Me Go With You

I watched a child run
and felt
an excitement for living.

I watched a child patiently
manipulate and explore
all that was around him,
and felt an appreciation
for curiosity.

I watched a child contemplate and act
upon a directive
from an adult
and felt a deep sense
of responsibility.

I watched a child cry
and felt
compassion.

I watched a child
imitate me
and felt a sense of power
to be channeled.

I watched a child playing
and decided to play too.

I watched a child run to me
and we walked
slowly,
hand in hand.

I watched a child
and learned
how to take time
to live.

My Puppy

At the welcoming trail
my puppy bounds ahead eagerly.
My stride lengthens to match hers.
Shoulders ease,
as my gaze relaxes
on the sun-filtered green before me.
She gambols back
with a playfulness in her eyes
and trots along side for a while.
Off again,
to catch up
with a drifting smell or sound.
She forces me
to keep my perceptions comfortable.
Look down too long,
and I miss the brilliant blue of the sky
peeking through the shimmering leaves.
Look up too long,
and a gnarled root or projecting rock
nestled in the path
trips up my foot.
My little friend
is swiftly at my side again,
reassuringly.

Happy Motion

The puppy
bounding and running
with its friend
the child…
a bundle
of happy motion

Mon Chat

It pleases me
that when I
press you gently to my cheek
you are not too disdainful.
Rather
you purr,
and allow me,
for a while,
to intrude upon your
dignity.

You Are Dying.

I see your body aging,
your energy and strength dwindling.
The light in your eyes glows softly
rather than brightly.

I know that the you
who is known to me
is going to die.

How do I prepare myself?
How do I walk with you
as you ready to leave?
How shall we sit
when the time comes?

Shall we hold hands
and gaze together,
wordlessly,
across the time
that has come and gone?

Many sunsets and storms
have passed through your life,
many cycles of moons and seasons.
You have watched me come
and go and return again.

What blessing can be adequate
for me to utter
as you breath your last breath?

As my heart shatters
under the strain of letting go,
will I have the strength
to sing with your soul,
as it flies free
to the unknowable
All Knowing One?

If I cannot be present
when you pass from here,
breathe a whisper on the wind
to my ear,
that I may know where you are.

But, if I am fortunate enough
to be with you,
let us both be brave
and face
the terrifying wonder
together
with joyful psalm!

Death in the Garden

When one has lived long and fully,
had time to bloom and create seed
for future life,
when one has had time to age,
to slow, to whither and dim,
the expected visit from God's Hand of Death
is welcomed as part of the natural cycle.
We are missed. We are mourned.
We are let go and blended
with rich memories.

But when one is taken unexpectedly,
at the fullness of bloom,
or even before the blossoming begins,
the expectant promise made empty
is wretchedly felt by those who stare
at the empty space.
The color, the scent, the texture
is gone too soon, irretrievably gone.
The shock shakes the foundation of faith,
and grief walks with despair.
For there are no answers from the Gardener
who has cut the flower so soon.

Only when we have walked for a while
holding the Hand of Death,
leaving the door open
for anguish to come and go,
only when we have kept our hearts open
to the acknowledgment of a purpose
greater than our individual lives,
when we have cried out our sorrow and
let the tears mingle with the grief of all
who mourn through time,
then may we see the void filled with a gift
that would not otherwise
have been received.

The loss is not lessened.
But somehow, in time,
room is made for more,
for something new,
perhaps unexpected and inexplicable.
It may be that only God knows
that it is in memorium.

Life and Death

The birds are singing loudly.
They don't know that someone has died!
The sun rises gloriously,
casting pinks and gold across the sky.
It is unaware that our hearts grieve today.
The breeze dances with the flowers in the garden.
It passes over our tears without lingering.
No. Life does not pause to weep with Death.
It springs from it, again and again.
It seems to be humanity's plight to anguish so,
though none knows why.

Death's Blessing

As you take care of necessary details,
you may reflect upon a life
that has lived its time here.
Sadness may swell to fill
the opening space created by loss.
May this space then be filled with memories
which lead to a warm inner smile.
May you be blessed with the peace
that comes with knowing Love.
In the realm of prayers, where all roads meet,
and where listens the Greatest Love,
you will continue to know one another.

82

<u>My Birthday</u>

Many years
with their varied seasons
have come and gone,
and once again
it is my birthday.
This time,
my heart beats with great joy,
for now I know
how old
I really am.

I am as old as the mountains
reaching high into the clouds
with dust crumbling at the base.

I am as young as the new stream
bubbling up from the earth
to cascade over the rocky slope.

I was born
many uncountable
ages ago
and am born again
this day.

Life in the Garden

At the corner of the cement path through my garden,
there is a tiny patch of hard, rocky soil
ringed by creeping phlox.
The runoff of rain periodically surges
through this seemingly desolate patch.

After the phlox has shed its rich color,
having had its turn in glory,
there is a pause.
Then, as the days continue to warm,
a small shoot of green pokes through
that hard, rocky spot.

Bravely, earnestly, with a special mission
of bringing the color of the brilliant blue summer sky
to hover over the corner of cement path,
a small bunch of forget-me-nots blooms.
There, their resilience and brilliance
greets my passing daily.
It is a joy to my heart.

Now that winter is once again on the wane,
I look forward to the special promise
of life in that tiny rocky patch.
I pray that it is again able to return
to reflect here below
the radiance of color seen above.

The Journey for Spiritual Family

If one is born fortunate enough to be taught a theology, with its accompanying symbols, prayers, and traditions for communing with God and expressing joy, there is a foundation from which to go out into life seeking more. It may be that the questioning and searching brings one back to one's roots. Then the return is seen with greater clarity and is a decision based upon real understanding rather than upon family loyalty.

However, it may also happen that the exploration causes one to abandon the childhood teachings. This is a great loss, akin to a death, leaving a deep void. The emptiness fills with a longing to reconnect, to find again what has been lost. The search for new words and meanings, for a people with whom to travel and practice new traditions, is a long one. There are many doors opened, many teachers met, old and new masters with wisdom to impart. Varied symbols and rituals are tried, different songs sung and prayers heard. From each, some small part may be absorbed and taken for one's own. But, such a mixed collection is difficult to unify into a meaningful whole.

The struggle continues until the emptiness is accepted. Sitting there, with no meaning to know, the present moment is all that there is. Seeing only the beauty of each tree, and of every star on a clear night, traveling within the cycles of the moon, giving thanks for the blessings of having dishes to wash and someone to smile at, the longing is acknowledged and let go. No longer searching, no longer trying to fill the void with anything in particular, just being in it is enough. It is as if one travels down through a deep, dark, moist cave and finds there at the bottom, the river of Love and Compassion. Here are reflected the faces of the world all around.

Somewhere in that world is the spirit of someone never before met. You see the eyes of ancestors from a time before time, from a nation no longer known, from a history and tradition different from that into which you were born. Immediately you sense a deep kinship that crosses all boundaries of time and family. Within its story lies a symbol whose meaning resonates with your Soul, a ritual whose image quickens a long hidden remembrance. Together they strike a chord that is familiar to the song in your heart.

The void bursts with recognition, throwing wide the door leading to the people, tradition, prayer and song for which you have been searching. Your renewed life is once again filled with meaning, purpose and expression. The boundless joy that is felt is filled with awe and the dance of homecoming is begun!

Visiting Judy

"When do you want to go home?"
the doctor asked me.
"I didn't want to come in the first place!"
I snapped.
They did a good job.
Staples will come out soon.
But now I have a fever.
A clot stuck somewhere.

It's all right.
It's all right.
It has to be, you see.

I'm sorry it's this way.
But my body doesn't work right anymore.
And here I am
in a place where I don't want to be.
I have no control over any of it.
But I'm getting used to being this way.

It's all right.
It's all right.
This is the way things are.

Life's been a bunch of crises,
one after another.
I battled and I scrambled.
I tried to make the right choices.
I'm tired now.
I'd like a longer rest in between.

It's all right.
It's all right.
It has to be, you see.

Don't know where I'm going next.
Don't know who will take care of me.
I'll figure out something.
This, too, will pass you see.
Somehow it'll work out.
But right now I can't think.

It's all right.
It's all right.
This is the way things are.

My body's hot.
The fever drives me crazy.
I can't stand this.
I want to yell and scream.
I don't feel like being nice right now.
I have to make someone listen.

It's all right.
It's all right.
It has to be, you see.

I don't have any faith.
I don't understand God.
But when the Rabbi chanted for me
I felt a connection from far away.
Something very ancient soothed me.
it's hidden in my veins.

It's all right.
It's all right.
This is the way things are.

I wonder if my life
has been any good.
Yet I did the best I could.
Thank you for coming.
I am tired now.
I am drifting,
falling asleep again.

> . . . Kiss her cheek.
> Wings of Shechina,
> please fan her brow.
> . . . Leaving quietly,
> her mantra fills my head:

It's all right.
It's all right.
It has to be, you see.
It's all right.
It's all right.
This is the way things are.

Gates

Having found your family,
your prayers,
your songs,
take delight in them.
May they guide your path
and fill your spirit.
Yet, beware.
Let them not be as a fence
around your life,
nor a lock
on your heart.
Remember....
The Gates to the One
are not defined
or fully illuminated
by any one way.
All who seek
may find a path
to the Unity that Is.
As you pray,
keep your heart open
so that your song
may find harmony with others.
For the One is with All,
and all may come to know
the One.

Beyond Faith

Beyond faith
is the sense of oneness
with all that is.

An awareness
of that which cannot be named
or fully known
fills the smallest moment
with awe.

Knowing that every movement
or thought
participates immediately
in the miracle of co-creating
fills me with responsibility
and compassion.

The work of mending the world
is contained
in every breath.

Every thought, every action
is a conversation
with G-d,
and an opportunity
to raise sparks
of light.

The Throne of God

I grew up on images
of the throne of G-d
painted with brilliant light
filled with an angelic realm
singing praises and glory.

But I have learned
that there cannot be light
without darkness;
and the brighter the light,
the blacker the dark depths.

And so I say
that the throne of G-d
can equally be found
in the darkest of dark,
in the deepest stillness
where not a breath is heard.

Around the Throne
in the Great Night
the first glimmer of light
sparkles with an extraordinary glow,
and the softest sound,
escaping with the first breath,
is the sound of awe.

The Last Day of My Life

Let me look to this day
as the last day of my life.
Let me notice the sun sparkling
through the dewdrop on the small blade of grass,
watch the slow unfurling of the blossom
in the early morning sun,
hear the bird's song on the breeze.

Let me look to this day
very carefully,
so that my soul may leave
with a remembrance of the beauty
that fills the earth.

Let me lift the head of the homeless one,
wipe a tear,
hold the rage of someone's fear,
so that my soul may leave
with a remembrance of compassion.

Let me look long
into my beloved's eyes
as we sit together in the quiet
of the nothing that is All,
so that my soul may leave
with a remembrance of love.

Let me look to this day
as the last day of my life,
for it is holy.

94

With Wings

With the wings of Shechina,
gather sparks of light
from the dark night sky
and sprinkle them below
to brighten each soul.
Send the music of Miriam
soaring on the wind
to fill each heart with song.
Dance now!
Elijah comes!

Like A Rose

Life is like a rose,
slowly unfurling.
Breath deeply of the sweet scent
while handling the thorns with care.
Life, like the rose,
is a psalm
from G-d to you,
and from you back to G-d.

Crossing

You are gone now,
irretrievably gone.
With you, too, has passed
a part of my life,
never to be lived again.

I had to let you go
where I could not follow,
and heavy tears choke my spirit.

I remain in the world
of time and opposites,
while you have gone on
to Timelessness
and Unity.

Yet I know
where we can meet,
though hands cannot touch,
and eyes cannot see.

It is a sacred space,
a bridge
that spans
unseen worlds.

If I am very still,
I can pause
at the center.

There I can open to you
and receive
within my heart
the love that
sustains me
until I too can cross
and be again
wholly with you.

When I Die

When I die,
do not grieve for me,
for I shall be dancing with
the wind on the crest of the sea,
glittering in the starlight,
shimmering on the sands.
Do not grieve for me,
for I shall be
in the embrace
of all there is to be.

If tears flow,
and your heart aches,
so let it be.
Grieve, but grieve
with joy for me,
and know that I have lived
each of my days fully.

Go, stand by the sea,
and close your damp eyes.
Sit with your sorrow,
letting it flow through you
with the song of the waves.
Turn your cheek to the breeze.
With it
I shall kiss you gently,
with the deepest of love
that ever could be.

For, lo,
though you cannot touch my lips,
and you cannot catch my laugh,
I shall be surrounded and filled by
the greatest of all love,
the Source of All Life,
and able to embrace you within me
as forever
as the sand and the sea.

Divinity

Divinity shines in the stars and the opening rose.
It fills gratitude and joy in the company of love.
But how do I understand
the whereabouts or purpose of Divinity
in the faces of those who are lost and confused,
poor and destitute, downtrodden and heartbroken?

Listening in the night,
I hear it whispered that they are here
so that I might know and act
with compassion.

Look past the lost light of their eyes,
beyond their broken spirits. There,
you can see the spark of Divinity,
lying within, waiting to be nourished and freed.

But harder it is, I think,
to see the spark of God
in the hand of the murderer,
those who rape and kill,
those whose anger, fear and prejudice
lead to genocide.

Often have I pondered this,
while absent-mindedly busy with this and that.
Then it came to me suddenly,
shaking the very core of my being.
My body trembled. My breath paused. I froze.

In the light of day,
I heard the voice whisper,
"They are here so that you may know and act
with forgiveness."

Even deep in those angry, frightened eyes,
under the rage and the terror,
the spark of the Holy One is buried. Waiting.
These souls are perhaps the greatest of all,
who have come to suffer thus,
so that you may know and act.

I am dizzy with the thought.
For to choose compassion and forgiveness
is at once both terrifying and meaningful.

Have those brave ones separated from
the knowledge of their Holiness
to slip into darkness
that we may learn to recognize their Source
and go to meet them?

Have they covered their sparks
with that which we have hidden away
in our own depths, unclaimed,
that we may learn
to recognize ourselves?

Courageous are those souls
who descend into the reaches
of depression, rage, greed, and fear,
so that those who see them
can come to know and understand.

Yet to forgive does not mean to forget,
but to remember.
Remember
that here, on this earth,
our human perspective
is of duality and division.

But with God, All is One.
The only Truth
is the One that unites us all.
We are they,
and they are we.
Unity can occur
only when both are known.

The call to all is to remember.
Remember
to repair the world,
inner and outer,
with compassion and forgiveness.

102

Then, too, what of those times
when we ourselves experience suffering,
loss, anger and grief,
plagued by fear and doubt?

Is it so that we may come to know
the wisdom of God
and so grow in faith?
Are we to accept the vicissitudes of life
without understanding them?

I hear the whisper:
"That is
understanding.
Being secure
in not knowing
is
knowing."

So walk with me now
at the edge of the turbulent sea.
Feel the stillness in the dark depths below.
There is no voice whispering.
There is only Being.
And remember,
Being is sacred.

A Different Kind of Love

You I love with a different kind of love.
There are no words for it.
It is simply there.
I do not own it or control it.
It flows its own course,
rising from a deep warm place
as a spring from the depths of the earth.

Where it journeys to, or how far,
I do not know.
It delights in the mystery of its being,
while acknowledging the reality of longing.

It is not expressed with caresses
or sweet murmurings,
but felt with a fullness of the heart
in appreciation for Your presence.

The passion of a storm at the edge of the sea
thrills me.
The delicacy of a butterfly fluttering near
fills me with awe.
Breathing deeply the scent of a rose
soothes my spirit.
The love that my beloved whispers in my ear
warms my heart.

But, You I love with a different kind of love.
I cannot speak it; I can only dance it.
I dance it alone,
to the rhythm of my heart beat,
letting it course through my body
fluidly, softly, steadily.

Becoming one with its rhythm,
I feel life and longing blend.
Re-connecting with my soul,
the inexpressible love
Is released
and I am again whole.

D'Varim

Enough!

When I hear the Voice whisper, "It is enough,"
then true comfort, true rest,
true Shabbos is reached.
And, perhaps, that is the new land to be given to me,
a new land to conquer and walk on now,
as one with HaShem.
No more struggles,
no more battles to be won,
letting G-d alone be the judge.

When the work is done,
it is time to teach others,
it is time to stop and let others go on.
Imbue them with strength.
Their lands to conquer and possess
will be different from mine.
Teach them how G-d can be,
will be, is
in their midst.
Fear not becoming old,
of letting go,
of stopping.
It has been "Enough!"

How awesome
that these Words
have come to me at this time of my life,
when the hair is white
and the body failing.

My time of wandering
was passed long ago.
The conquering of fears,
the learning to listen,
has been on-going.
Now, is the final fear,
the fear of stopping,
the fear of ending,
to be conquered too?

Blessed is the One who says
that I am "enough!"

(Inspired by Deuteronomy 3:26)

Shema, Yisrael

Shema, Yisrael!
Did you hear it?
A Word has been spoken.
It floats on a breath
from the silence,
from the stillness,
from the nothing.

Listen, Yisrael,
from that place deep within
where you struggle with the Divine.
Be still and listen.
Breathe with the One Breath.
Hear the One Sound,
the One that is All.
Be still and come to know
the spark
that remembers its Source.

Bind as a sign upon your hand…
Know, Yisrael,
that if you reach out with open hands,
you may receive and give
in partnership with the Divine.

Visible before your eyes…
If you see with wonder
when you look,
you may recognize
the Unity of All Life.

Shema, Yisrael.
Inscribe this memory, this knowing,
on the door posts to your hearts
and on the gates of your lives,
on those places from which
you come and go,
those places which sometimes close up
with fear and confusion.
Inscribe them there
so they may be flung open
with love.

The Love that is Boundless
and Timeless,
that flows on the Breath
that spoke the Word
that our Souls hear.
This is the promise
inscribed on the mezuzah,
on the door posts which frame our lives,
by the One who breathes
through eternity,
when we stop to listen and to hear.

(Inspired by Deuteronomy 6:4-9)

Blessings

Blessed be your sorrow, for with you
I may learn to weep.
Blessed be your pain, for with you
I may learn to empathize.
Blessed be your hunger, for with you
I may learn to nourish.
Blessed be your fear, for with you
I may learn to reach out.
Blessed be your loneliness, for with you
I may learn to embrace.
Blessed be your weakness, for with you
I may learn to be patient.
Blessed be your differences, for with you
I may learn to be tolerant.
Blessed be your suffering, for with you
I may learn to take action.
Blessed be your rage, for with you
I may learn to see my own.
Blessed be my own, for with it
I may learn forgiveness.
Blessed be your silence, for with you
 I may learn to be still.
Blessed be your strength in adversity,
for with you I may learn courage.
Blessed be your life, for with you
I may learn wisdom.
Blessed be your divinity, for with you
I may learn to be complete.

110

Blessed be the strength of the Earth
that brings forth storms,
for it teaches me humility.
Blessed be the power of the Earth
to regenerate,
for it teaches me healing.
Blessed be our joy, for together
we celebrate God.
Blessed be our prayers, for heart felt
they sing to God.
Blessed be our lives,
for through them
God sings to us.
Blessed be the Almighty All Knowing
for giving the cycles
and passages of Life.
Blessed be....

The Dream

One clear, dark night, a dreamer entered the Dream time and began a journey. The road led to a large hall filled with elders, the sages, the wise people. It seemed to be a long ago time and a far away place, for they were dressed in robes that flowed to their feet, with hats or shawls covering their heads. Each was standing at a lectern, all in a great circle, involved in intense discussion. There was an empty lectern waiting for the dreamer. There were priests, rabbis, monks, astrologers, scientists, philosophers, each one making a presentation, debating a truth, each from their own perspective. The dreamer stood at the empty lectern, listening. Lively words flew back and forth, from one to another, as each pointed out this or that to be so. Then, suddenly, they all turned to the watching dreamer, expecting a response. There was a pause. Then the dreaming one spoke, softly, but with great clarity, saying simply, "The truth is the truth is the truth, and the only truth that is, is God."

At the very moment that the words were uttered, in a flash, gone was the great hall, as the dreamer woke with a start.....filled with awe!

God is All There Is,
and All There Is,
Is Now.

Blessed Are They

Blessed are they
who are able
to replace fear
with understanding.

Their lives fill
with tranquillity.

Aware of their unity
with All,
no dogma or ritual
is needed,
only holy being.